The Essential Little Book of Great Lawyering

By
JAMES A. DURHAM

Published by James A. Durham
902 High Street
Dedham, MA 02026

Publisher's Cataloging-in-Publication Data
Durham, James A.

The essential little book of great lawyering : what every lawyer needs to do to succeed / by James A. Durham. – Dedham, MA : James. A. Durham, 2006, revised and reprinted, 2009.

p. ; cm.
ISBN: 0-9773131-0-7
ISBN13: 978-0-9773131-0-5

1. Lawyers. 2. Attorney and client. 3. Success in business.
I. Title.

K117 .D87 2005
340/.023-dc22   2005909538

Printed in the United States of America
10 09 08 07 06 • 5 4 3 2 1

Contents

Prologue

The words that follow are an attempt to synthesize over 20 years of experience as a businessperson, lawyer and consultant. This book is designed to combine a poignant discussion about the legal marketplace with a candid description of the fundamental skills that are required to be successful as a lawyer. This modest book will give you all of the insights you need to respond to the ever-changing opportunities and challenges that confront you every day in your legal practice.

If there is one principle that I try to employ in all of my speaking and writing, it is to take information that appears to be complex, and reduce it to something understandable and practical. I try to take the overwhelming and make it feel manageable. Another goal of any work I do is to deliver information in a context that is relevant to the specific audience. Accordingly, this material is presented with a sensitivity to the real challenges that lawyers face in trying to meet client and firm demands, develop new business and lead a fulfilled personal life. Much is required of lawyers as they try to meet the sometimes onerous expectations of a changing professional environment, but if you understand the principles in this book, you will increase the likelihood of success (and even have some fun along the way).

I am not a "business-school type," nor have I spent any time working in public relations or psychology, for that matter. What I bring to this discussion is the real-world perspective that comes from my experience as both a practicing lawyer and a purchaser of legal services. Also, I know what I know from having talked to hundreds of clients who work with lawyers on a broad array of legal work. Finally, I have worked with hundreds of lawyers and law firms as a coach, trainer, and consultant.

I am driven by a genuine desire to help lawyers enhance their practices and improve their lives. With all of the reported discontent in our profession, it is important to look for ways in which we can make the experience of practicing law more positive, fulfilling, and successful.

I am confident that what I have written

here will help you do that. If nothing else, this book will help you address many of the real-world issues that confront you in your day-to-day practices.

Chapter 1
Setting the Stage for Greatness

I struggled for a long time to come up with a title for this book. Since great lawyers inevitably attract, keep, and grow clients, I was tempted to call it *The Essential Little Book of Business Development*—or maybe even—*The Essence of Selling Legal Services*. That might have been a good idea from a promotional standpoint, since most lawyers want to learn how to "get business." And there is a movement in the legal profession to teach lawyers so-called "sales" skills.

But if I have learned one thing in my experience as a lawyer, consultant, and trainer, it is that lawyers typically have serious misconceptions about how they should "sell" legal services. They think of business development as an unseemly proposition; they see it as an exercise in which they *push* themselves and their firms on people who don't need or want what they have to offer. If that were an accurate description of how you should *sell* legal services, I would not want any part of it either. Fortunately, that approach is just plain wrong.

Moreover, most lawyers want to believe that ***just being a great lawyer is enough to help them achieve all of their business development goals***. Since being a great lawyer is what this book is about, let me say right up front that I agree with the maxim that **Being a great lawyer IS the best business development plan**.

> The problem with this approach, however, is that lawyers want to define "great lawyers" in terms they understand, when what really matters is how clients define "great lawyers."

Being a great lawyer always leads to client loyalty, client growth, and referrals—which means new business.

Put another way, my work has revealed that the most important qualities of successful lawyers are about service and attitude; the quality of their drafting or their negotiating skills are not sufficient to distinguish great lawyers from everyone else.

Don't get me wrong, many rainmakers are *also* seen as great technical or procedural lawyers. But almost all lawyers are good at the law. Lawyers are overwhelmingly viewed as *great* by clients *for other reasons*. Since no one ever taught us these client-focused qualities in law school (or in the early years of our careers as lawyers), my hope is that this book will fill the void.

Early in our careers as lawyers we are taught what it takes to be called a great lawyer *within a law firm*: excellent research and writing skills, good negotiation and organization skills, consistent demonstration of scholarly insight and a thoughtful (dare I say "innovative") approach to solving legal problems. While there is certainly value in being recognized by your colleagues as a savvy technical lawyer, a terrific advocate, or a superb writer, these are — or should be — the skills of *all* lawyers!

To achieve true greatness you must do all of these things, and more. Understanding what makes clients see you as a great lawyer is what this book is about.

In writing this book, I kept coming back to this question: "In order to truly be successful in this profession, what do lawyers need to learn beyond what is taught in law school and in the early years of practice?" The answer seemed too simple to be true, but it is the right answer: Lawyers need to learn that ***it is the overall experience clients have working with them that will determine their success***.

Lawyers in private practice exist to serve clients—not to serve the firms in which they are employed, not to feed their egos, not to satisfy intellectual curiosity, and not to fill their bank accounts. Like a doctor, plumber, architect, or teacher, we are expected to know the substantive information, rules, and laws of our profession; we are expected to possess the skills needed to do what the profession demands. But it is how we treat the people we represent, and the attitudes we bring to our work, and the value clients perceive in our relationship that will determine whether we are great lawyers.

So, if our success really flows from what clients think about us, it would be good to have a clear understanding of what impresses them. We need to know what makes clients hire us, what causes them to continue to work with us, what motivates them to give us additional work, and what makes them refer other people to us.

Let's be honest, whether someone has

practiced law for many years or they are new to the legal profession, their future success will be tied closely to their ability to attract, serve, keep, and grow business. Achieving success and a reputation as a great lawyer does not come from clever marketing; it is not about your law school class rank or your LSAT scores or how smart you are. It is about your skills in dealing with clients. Accordingly, I settled on *The Essential Little Book of Great Lawyering* as a title for this book.

> This book is intended to give you a road map to success by articulating what a lawyer needs to do to have every client say:
> *"My lawyer is the best lawyer with whom I have ever worked."*

Not every person who has passed a bar exam has the innate skills to be a great lawyer, but almost anyone can learn them—and they must. The communication, relational, and attitudinal skills that are essential to being a great lawyer are just as important as being able to name the most relevant Supreme Court decisions.

What is my definition of success as a lawyer? You are a great lawyer when, in addition to knowing the law, you have become a lawyer that people trust above all others, and you are the person to whom they turn when they (or people they know) have any kind of problem.

I am tempted to say that this book is little more than a systematic application of common sense. (Hey, there is another potential title!) But if we, as lawyers, can simply "do unto clients as we would have other professionals do unto us," we would all be great lawyers.

When you hire an accountant, a landscaper, or a financial planner to do work for you, what would your reaction be if they did not return your phone calls promptly or failed to ask you important questions about what you expect and what you want to accomplish? What if there were no personal connection and they did not seem the least bit interested in you personally? What if they did not get things done when they said they would, and they sent you a bill for more than you expected to pay? What if they were working on an hourly rate basis, but seemed to have no concern at all for efficiency and had no creative strategies to minimize the time needed for the project? For many lawyers, this list of behaviors is only modestly troubling. For clients, however, these behaviors characterize *ordinary* lawyers, not great ones.

We may have come to expect these less-than-impressive behaviors from many of the people we hire, but that does not justify a belief that these behaviors are acceptable.

Service cannot take a back seat to brains in the quest to be an outstanding lawyer. While being smart is essential, if it were sufficient for greatness, almost every lawyer would be an incredible success. Giving clients true value and an incredible experience is what being great is all about.

Some of my consultant friends have suggested that if I achieve the goal of writing the definitive practical book on client service for lawyers, it might put them out of business. As someone who recently left the consulting world to work with a terrific law firm, that prospect is less disconcerting than it used to be.

> If we can get lawyers to appreciate that it is more important to care about clients than it is to add an extra billable hour to their day, then we might actually be able to eliminate lawyer jokes in our lifetime. If every lawyer would read, digest, and live the principles in this book, there would, in fact, be no more lawyer jokes.

Moreover, if I can change the attitudes and behaviors of individual lawyers by writing this book, then consultants can turn their attention to helping firms develop better internal support and mentoring programs; implement better client communication systems; create operational and compensation systems that promote client service; and encourage better personal growth and creativity for lawyers and staff.

The first article I published as a legal marketer appeared in *The American Lawyer* magazine in 1997. It was entitled: "Stop Thinking Like a Lawyer." Now, after many years of working with lawyers and their clients, I still cannot give you any better advice.

If you want to be a great lawyer, then you must think like clients think. You must put yourself in the shoes of a client and ask: What would I want to have happen right now? What would I want this lawyer to ask me if I were the client? What information would I want from the lawyer so I could feel comfortable about having them represent me? What demeanors and attitudes is he or she conveying to give me confidence that I have the right lawyer working for me? What feedback would I want the lawyer to seek from me? How would I like the work to be coordinated and managed? What would I want this lawyer to know about my business?

These are the things we need to start

thinking about if we want to be great lawyers. Our success as lawyers is determined *in equal parts* by *what we do* **and** *how we do it*.

My friend Tom Sager asked me to make one more point when he reviewed this book. Tom is SVP and General Counsel – DuPont Legal, where he helped pioneer the DuPont Convergence and Law Firm Partnering Program; so he understands the importance of good service. Tom was concerned, however, that the book put so much emphasis on the strength of personal relationships (and the concept of making your client "look good"), that we could lose sight of the fact that, in representing a business, the company is the ultimate client.

We can all use a reminder that in our zeal to provide great personal service to the people who hire us, we must be willing to give the hard, sound advice that is sometimes needed to help the organization – even when that advice is not necessarily in the best interest of the individuals with whom we work. Done right, this is yet another example of great lawyering.

Chapter 2
The Essence of Great Lawyering

In order to be a great lawyer, you need to know the perceived level of importance clients attach to the work you do for them. You can disagree with a client's characterization of what you are doing, but at the end of the day, it's what the client thinks that matters.

Most law firm marketing materials say something like: "We have extensive expertise and experience providing cost-effective legal services on a wide variety of matters with a sensitivity to client needs and relationships." That pretty much covers all of the bases—but it means nothing. Every lawyer and law firm makes these same claims, and for much of the work that lawyers do for clients, some of these alleged benefits are actually irrelevant.

Clients describe the work lawyers do as falling into three categories: *commodity, important,* or *bet-the-company*.

For commodity work, the driving factor in selection and client satisfaction is cost. Doing the work with no hassles for the client and being responsive are good, but it is really all about having the lowest price. Accordingly, if the client perceives the work as commodity work, you are wasting your time talking about expertise, teamwork, and relationship-building. If you are doing this type of work, your primary goal must be to do it efficiently and inexpensively.

At the other end of the spectrum is so-called "bet-the-company" work. When a client is facing a problem that could lead to jail time or the end of their business, the *only thing* that matters in choosing and judging a lawyer is expertise. Cost-saving efforts and relationship building will not determine client satisfaction. It's all about the result. Certainly, if you do bet-the-company work while being nice and keeping cost down, that will never hurt you, but it is not where you should focus your efforts.

I have learned from talking to hundreds of clients and lawyers that clients perceive about

25% to 30% of the work lawyers do generally to be commodity (using my definition that the *exclusive* selection criteria for the work is price). For some clients the percentage of perceived commodity work might be 90%, and for others 10%, so it is critical to know what each client thinks, but generally, it is about one-third of all available legal work. Bet-the-company work represents only about 5% of the available legal work in the marketplace. While some problems have broad implications and the results would have a meaningful impact on a company, they seldom rise to the level of "business life-or-death."

> When lawyers are performing **important** work for clients, the drivers of satisfaction can be as varied as the personalities and operational structures of the clients.

That means that the bulk of the work that lawyers do falls into a third category of work: the "important" category. To be great lawyers, we must understand what matters most to clients when handling their important work. In this category of work, success turns on how clients are treated.

When you are doing *important* legal work your expertise and competence must be

sufficient (but need not be exceptional), and the billing rates or projected costs for the work must be within the range of client expectations (but not necessarily the lowest). Beyond that, the key to client satisfaction is what it is like to work with you; your success will be determined by the actual experience a client has working with you. Ultimately, a client evaluates a lawyer's performance for important work by asking: "Is this lawyer someone with whom I want to work?"

What impresses one client may be that you have "a strong number two" on the client service team, or that you offer an easily understandable billing format; for another client you are their best lawyer because you provide them with legal updates that they can pass along to management, or you let them use the firm's stadium box for a child's birthday party. Another client is thrilled that you give them a weekly e-mail update on the status of all matters, or that you regularly bring members of the legal team to their office (at no cost) to meet the people on the client's staff.

When it comes to doing important work, one size does not fit all. There are, however, certain fundamental service attributes that **all** great lawyers understand. I have studied successful lawyers and I have checked my findings with clients to determine precisely what the common characteristics of great lawyers are. The good news is that these characteristics of great lawyers can be emulated by all lawyers.

Whenever I conduct a client interview, the first question I always ask is "What do you like best about working with the firm?" The answer almost every time is that the primary lawyer "is really responsive and really *knows my business*." Think about this for a moment. In over 175 meetings with clients, that is the answer I get about 90% of the time. In the face of that data, how can we think that anything is more important to a lawyer's professional reputation than being responsive and knowing the client's business? Business clients of every shape, size, and industry want the same basic things from their lawyers.

Technically, *what* we do as lawyers is, *inter alia*, write contracts, give legal advice, negotiate, litigate disputes, and assist with regulatory compliance. We must do these things well to be successful, but almost all lawyers do. *How* we do this work—responsively, and with an understanding of the client's needs and business—is where we need to focus if we want to be perceived as great lawyers. But there is more.

Chapter 3
The Common Characteristics of Great Lawyers

Great lawyers clearly do *not* have the same personality type, work style, nationality, gender, age, or practice area. So there is real value in uncovering what they do that leads to their success.

To help understand what makes lawyers successful, I talked to lawyers who were introverts and extroverts; I talked to high-powered litigators and understated business lawyers. I selected successful lawyers whose personalities and styles were very different, because I was tired of being told that getting and keeping and growing clients was essentially a "personality contest."

I also checked with clients generally to make sure that the common characteristics I found in these lawyers were the characteristics that clients truly valued in their best lawyers. The results are unequivocal and are set forth below.

Be Responsive and Accessible

Remember the point I made earlier: Being responsive and knowing a client's business are *always* part of a client's description of a great lawyer. I have had clients tell me in client interviews that the importance of responsiveness cannot be underestimated. One client said, "The importance of responsiveness cannot be overstated; as clients we are almost irrationally consumed with our outside counsel's responsiveness." Clearly, you cannot be a great lawyer if you are not responsive.

It is critical, however, to know what *responsiveness* means to a client. Most lawyers think it means returning phone calls within some prescribed period of time—perhaps the same day or within an hour or two. In fact, responsiveness really means: (1) being accessible to clients, and (2) delivering documents (or answers or advice) when you say you will. Every great lawyer understands these two concepts and lives them.

And every client I have ever talked to has said these are essential qualities of great lawyers.

Accessibility means that the client can find you (or someone else who knows what is going on) whenever they need to. Anytime. Anywhere.

Many lawyers say they do not want clients to call them at home at night or on weekends; many say they do not like the fact that clients expect them to constantly be available for e-mail or calls. Others say they don't want any client interruptions while on a vacation or when spending time with their family. We all live with multiple obligations and need some down time. Unfortunately, to be an outstanding lawyer, you need to be available (or make clear arrangements for someone else with knowledge of the client to be available) to clients at all times.

> In the legal profession you can be a good or "OK" lawyer by returning phone calls reasonably quickly. To be a great lawyer you need to make yourself totally available.

When I was practicing law full time, I had one client that I represented on a variety of business matters. He not only asked me to do all of his legal work, but he also referred several new clients to me. I remember being sound asleep at home when he called once at 2 a.m. He was calling to tell me he was at the airport, and was having trouble getting his new nanny into the United States. (She was coming from Germany.)

He had not previously consulted me for immigration advice because he thought it was "no big deal." Some lawyers would resent this interruption, but I was actually glad to get the call. I value a good night's sleep as much as anyone, but I want clients calling me in that situation. If a client thinks you care enough to help solve a problem like this (and take a call at home at that hour) then you know you have developed the right kind of relationship with them.

Know the Client's Business

How well do you know your client's business? Can you answer questions such as: Who are their principal competitors? What is the potential market for their goods or services? How are the individuals at the client company rewarded or judged? What is the company's strategic plan? If you do not know these things, then you need to invest some time getting to know your clients better. You should do some meaningful research, and learn more about their business and what is important to them personally — that is the foundation for being considered a great lawyer.

One client told me that he would be willing to pay his lawyers to read his strategic plan, because it would make them more valuable to him. Another said she would be thrilled if her lawyers asked to read the company's strategic plan "but I wouldn't expect to pay them for it." A client in the retail business said she wanted to know that her lawyers have been to the company's stores, and that they understand how they introduced new merchandise.

In one clear example of the importance of knowing a client's business, a law firm made the mistake of asking for a rate increase just a day after the client (a public company) announced a bad first-quarter financial performance. The client said the firm might have been entitled to a fee increase, but the timing showed a lack of sensitivity and a lack of understanding of the client's business.

Research is useful, but the best way to learn about a client's business is to talk to them. You can learn a lot by just asking good questions and listening to the answers. This leads us to the next point: Communication is critical.

Communication Is the Secret to Success

Beyond being responsive and accessible and knowing the client's business, what else do great lawyers do? One of the common characteristics of great lawyers is that they *initiate contact* with clients (and others in their network). Great lawyers do not wait for their phones to ring—they make other people's phones ring; they do not wait for an e-mail from clients, they send them useful e-mails. Great lawyers do not wait for clients to ask for help, great lawyers know enough about the client to be able to call and suggest specific ways in which they might help—even before they are asked.

Helping a client be more successful means being able to assist them in one or more of the following four ways. Great lawyers *initiate contact* with clients to discuss how to:

> • help the client make money;
> • help the client save money;
> • help the client sleep better at night; and
> • make the client look good to superiors, peers, or colleagues.

Hundreds of clients have confirmed in meetings with me that lawyers who can make these things happen are great lawyers. For every client you work with, whether you are an associate working with a middle manager, or a partner dealing with a General Counsel, you need to be thinking about what you can do to make one of these things happen. (The middle manager you work with might sleep better, get a bigger bonus, or look good to the boss if you find a way to manage the litigation better, come up with a novel strategy to close deals in less time, or if you just keep them better informed about their matters so they have answers when their supervisor calls with questions.)

Providing "Value"

One of a client's best measures of a lawyer is whether or not they *add value* to the work and the relationship. Value means providing more than the basic legal work for which the client hired you.

> There should be a note on every lawyer's desk that says "What have I done today to make the people I am dealing with more successful and more comfortable?" Great lawyers appreciate the incredible level of communication needed to answer this question.

I have heard the word "value" described in many ways, but for a client working with a lawyer it almost always means: "I get something more than what I paid for."

If the legal work you did was competent, and the fee you charged was appropriate for the work, then (using this definition) the "value" would be zero. Providing a client with what they asked you to do is not a bad thing, but without more, the perceived value is minimal. In a competitive marketplace like the one in which lawyers practice, *you must provide more than simply that for which you were hired*.

For some clients, extra value can be found in helping them stay abreast of regulatory developments, or providing regular summaries of the status of matters, or helping their best friend get a job or tickets to an event. To another client, value comes from the fact that you spend time at their offices or have a great number-two lawyer on the team. For some people who do fast-paced deals, value is found in the fact that you are not constantly calling them for input and instructions; for someone else, it is the fact that you often seek their input. To know what your clients value, you must communicate regularly and clearly.

One increasingly important value proposition is effective matter management. Great lawyers keep the client informed of the progress and status of their matters (without overdoing it, or being a pest); they tell the client who is handling the work and when it will be done; and they make clear what the client needs to do to help the lawyer get a good outcome.

Almost all clients find value in lawyers who are on top of specific, relevant legal or industry developments that might impact their business strategy. They also value the opportunity to provide meaningful feedback, so long as the lawyers are willing to make adjustments to their service approach if the client asks for it.

Much of what it takes to add value to a client relationship takes only a few minutes a day. Lawyer value is not found in writing lengthy transmittal memos, doing extensive research or making speeches; it comes from calling, e-mailing, or visiting clients to learn what they are thinking. It means initiating contact to show that you care.

This latter point is particularly important when you are not actively working on a client matter. According to people who are supposed to know these things ("shrinks"), it takes seven contacts per year for someone to have you in mind when they need a lawyer, or need to refer someone to a lawyer. The biggest mistake I see among lawyers who are trying to build a practice and establish a great reputation, is that they do not initiate contact with or stay in touch with people for whom they have done work in the past.

The Personal Touch

Another fundamental aspect of great lawyering is recognizing the importance of *personalizing the relationship* to some degree. In almost every client interview I have ever done, the clients have said that it is important for their lawyers to be "people we like to work with." They want you to be someone with whom everyone at the client company (or family business or the association) likes to work. Personalizing the relationship does not mean that every client has to be your best friend; it does not mean you have to lavish them with fancy dinners or tickets. But clients make it very clear that "chemistry" matters.

You can start personalizing the relationship with something as simple as going to the client's place of business for an informal meeting or meal. It is hard to have a sense of what is going on in the client's life without seeing where he or she works and meeting some of the people with whom they work. If the client always comes to your office for meetings, you are missing a great opportunity to advance the relationship. This is not about "client entertainment," it is about having a personal connection with the

> Clients speak highly of lawyers who "understand the importance of relationships."

individuals with whom you do legal work.

I was facilitating a retreat for a group of associates at a law firm one Saturday, and there were four clients on a panel talking about what they value in lawyers. One of the panelists told the group a story that illustrates perfectly the importance of personalizing a client relationship.

He said that he met an associate for the first time at a closing dinner. During their brief conversation they discovered that they had a mutual interest in yachting. Several weeks after the dinner the client opened an envelope from the law firm and found an article about yachting that had been torn out of a flight magazine. An informal, handwritten note from the associate simply said: "I thought you might enjoy this."

The client said he immediately called the partner that was responsible for his work, to tell him he "wanted this associate to work on as many of his matters as possible." Clients— even busy executives and demanding in-house counsel—are real people (not billing categories). They appreciate a little personal attention.

Another in-house counsel said he wished

one of his outside lawyers would stop inviting him to attend professional basketball games. He said he liked basketball, but he didn't get to see his kids enough because of his busy schedule. "If the lawyer really knew me," he said, "he would know that I prefer not to be out on weeknights." He went on to say that he and his kids really like professional basketball, and it would be fine to offer him the tickets if the lawyer wanted to do something nice for him (subject to the company's gift-limitation policies, of course).

> Getting to know the personal interests, concerns, and desires of the people for whom you do legal work is essential.

Basically, great lawyers make an effort to connect personally with clients in a way that is appropriate for each client. For some clients, it is enough simply to remember to ask how their vacation went, or to send them your best recipe for their favorite type of food. For another, the appropriate personal touch is knowing that they need you to run interference with their boss. For some clients you show you care by sending them a book on a subject or by an author they care about; for others it is appropriate to offer to host their child's birthday party in the firm's luxury box.

The greatest complaint clients have about lawyers is that they do not listen. One of the best ways to improve listening skills is to better understand the whole human communication process. It is also helpful to stop talking; I am reminded of the simple phrase, "You can learn a lot just by listening."

Although it does not typically appeal to lawyers, it is important to seek out training programs that teach active listening, mirroring and matching body language, and understanding personality styles.

It amazes me how often lawyers in training programs have asked me what they should do to address certain client situations; they seem shocked when I tell them that it makes no sense to ask me—they should be asking the client (e.g., "Should I send them legal updates via e-mail or hard copy?" "How frequently should I update them on the status of the case?" "Is it better to call them before sending out a large bill, or address the reasons in a cover letter?").

To improve relationships and service, it is more important to spend time asking questions than it is to talk about yourself. Ask questions that help you uncover personal and professional needs and goals. Whenever you are unsure about something a client has said, or you just want to be sure you understand the point, one of the best active-listening questions is "Tell me what you mean by that." Another way to demonstrate excellent listening skills is to say, "Can you give me an example of that?"

You can also test your understanding of what a client has said by restating their words with your own interpretation. ("So, in other words, you don't think it's necessary to change the billing format.")

Great Lawyers Deliver

I have learned that great lawyers differ from most lawyers in that they are obsessed with keeping their promises. If they tell a client that they will have someone call them by Friday, they make sure the person calls by Friday. If they say they will have a document done by a certain time, it is done on time. In those rare instances when they cannot deliver on the promise, they call the client in advance to discuss it.

One in-house counsel I met told me that she fired her outside counsel "because they didn't deliver draft documents to her when they said they would, and they were sometimes rude to her secretary." They never missed a filing deadline or committed malpractice, but they lost a client with over $500,000 of annual billings primarily because they did not keep their basic promises.

The client said she always scheduled time to review pleadings and other documents from outside counsel. When her lawyers said they would get the documents to her by noon on Tuesday, she would set aside from noon to 2 p.m. to review the documents; when they arrived at 3:30 p.m. with a note saying they were needed by the next morning, it was a significant imposition.

One day she was complaining to her administrative assistant about the firm's performance, and the assistant said, "As long as you are complaining about them, I should tell you that they are sometimes rude when they call." At that point she made the decision to fire them. "It is easier to find a new law firm than it is to find a new secretary," she said. This supports so much of what has been said in these pages about service: Make clients comfortable, know their personal preferences and professional styles, and be responsive.

Confidence

Another important characteristic of great lawyers is that they project *confidence*. If you want clients to entrust you with their most important problems and challenges, you must appear to be confident. If you do not project confidence — indeed, if you do not have confidence in yourself — how can you expect a client to have confidence in you?

There is a fine line, however, between confidence and arrogance. Since "not listening" and arrogance are among the greatest complaints about lawyers, it would be a mistake to ignore this point about confidence. Many clients I interviewed told me that one of the most effective things a lawyer can do to impress them is to admit when they are wrong, or to acknowledge when their firm is not the best choice for a particular type of work. It demonstrates genuine confidence.

If you have any doubt about whether you project confidence or not, think about your presence at a closing or a drafting session. Do you arrive late, shuffle papers, and apologize for not having advanced your part of the project? When you are on time and prepared for the meeting, do you greet people with a solid (read: ordinary, not memorable) handshake, while looking them square in the eye and speaking clearly? Do you sit up straight and present yourself professionally during the course of the meeting? Do you project your voice when you are presenting, and avoid saying "um"? Do you listen carefully when others talk (not checking your wireless e-mail device constantly or working on documents)?

> Clients describe great lawyers as strong and respectful, and as people with whom they are proud to be associated.

The impression great lawyers make is one of being prepared and comfortable. Many clients describe their great lawyers as being "a presence" in a room—not necessarily commanding or dominating the room. This discussion of confidence reminds me of something my high school football coach always said: "Be proud, but be humble."

Loyalty to the Client

Another attitudinal quality that clients find in their best lawyers is loyalty—loyalty to the client that suggests that they will do anything they can to help their client succeed. Great lawyers give clients a sense that they will "do whatever it takes" (short of breaking the law, of course) to get the desired result. One client said, "I want my lawyers to be as concerned with my bottom line as they are with their own." Simply stated, clients believe their best lawyers are interested in helping them save money, make money, sleep better, or look good. More than one client has used the phrase "They've got my back covered."

This quality of loyalty is especially difficult to achieve in this era of expanding law practices, where requests for conflict waivers are increasing. It may be necessary for lawyers and firms to be more willing to align themselves with certain clients in industries with high concentrations of competition. Clients pay a lot of money to outside counsel, and more and more, they are asking for a greater measure of loyalty in return.

The client's feeling of loyalty largely flows from a lawyer's attitude. You want to have an attitude that lets clients know that you have adopted their problems. The client wants to know that you have taken *ownership* of their problems, and are committed unequivocally to doing everything that needs to be done to solve those problems

Chapter 4
Putting It All Together—A Summary of the Characteristics of Great Lawyers

Good lawyers return phone calls reasonably promptly; *great* lawyers are always available and accessible to their clients. *Great* lawyers don't just respond when their phone rings, they make other people's phones ring.

Good lawyers know the law; *great* lawyers know the law, but they also know and understand the client's business. *Great* lawyers know what makes the client successful and they understand the client's preferred form of communication.

Good lawyers get the legal work done. *Great* lawyers get the work done too, but they do it and give practical advice in the context of knowing the client's business.

Good lawyers do legal work effectively and efficiently. *Great* lawyers look for ways to make legal services more valuable to clients. *Great* lawyers give clients more than they pay for.

Good lawyers treat the client professionally. *Great* lawyers personalize the relationship by recognizing the unique styles, interests, and needs of the individuals with whom they work.

Good lawyers do their best to keep promises about when work will be completed. *Great* lawyers do what they say they will do, and get it done when they said they would. (In other words, *good* lawyers try to deliver, *great* lawyers DELIVER.)

Good lawyers are reasonably comfortable in most settings. *Great* lawyers project confidence, but not arrogance, in any setting. *Good* lawyers attend meetings; *great* lawyers arrive early—fully prepared. *Good* lawyers are present at meetings; *great* lawyers are a real *presence* in the meeting.

Good lawyers are thought of as "capable," and are expected to do a good job. *Great* lawyers own the client's problem, and engender a belief that they will do everything possible to help the client succeed.

Good lawyers care about clients. *Great* lawyers are loyal to them.

Good lawyers accept feedback when clients offer it. *Great* lawyers seek meaningful feedback from clients and act on it.

This is Not Just a Partner Primer

Just because you work with people at the client company who do not make the actual legal hiring decisions does not mean that you can give them minimal attention. The mid-level managers or junior in-house lawyers that rely on you for legal work today are the people who will shape your reputation as a lawyer now, and tomorrow.

It is critical to appreciate that the attributes of great lawyers described in this book are as applicable to an associate working with a middle manager as they are to a partner dealing with a General Counsel or senior executive.

For associates, the people you work with today will not only shape your reputation, but they can also have a significant impact on your career in other ways. They often take on greater responsibility within the organization, and they can take you with them by continuing to work with you at a higher level; they can move to another company where they have more power and influence over legal hiring; and they have friends who ask them for referrals. If you are a great lawyer, they will continue to work with you and refer new clients to you.

Be a Resource

Being a resource to your clients and other professionals makes you a better lawyer, too. Pay attention to the people in your network. It is well established in life and business that the more you give, the more you receive. Lawyers who refer people to others in their network get more referrals from that network. Why?

Making referrals among people in your network shows that you care about them, and it keeps you in an easily accessible place in their minds; also, it helps you stay in touch with what is going on in their lives and business. All of this leads people to want to do business with you.

The attitudes and skills discussed

throughout this book are important in dealing with all of your professional acquaintances, not just clients. That includes potential clients whom you know to be well served by other lawyers or firms. Indeed, there are many developments that could cause someone who is already represented by counsel to hire you in the future:

- Their existing firm could have a conflict.
- They may have new legal needs and their current firm can't handle them.
- Repeated service or performance failures by their current firm can lead to dissatisfaction, which causes them to *try* another lawyer or firm.
- Someone asks them for a referral and their current firm can't do it (or they decide to refer it to you just because they like you).
- A major change occurs at the person's current law firm:
    - A key lawyer leaves or retires.
    - The firm merges or breaks up.
    - The firm restructures its service team, billing rates, etc.
- A major change occurs in the potential client's business (a merger/acquisition, a management shake-up, reorganization, etc.), which changes the decision-making

process.

- You get to know the prospect well enough to suggest specific solutions to their problems—solutions that their existing lawyers have not uncovered.

To be a resource, you need to know not only the needs, skills, and values of the people in your network, but you also need to know the skills and experience of the people in your firm. What types of work do they do well? What industries are they strong in and what types of personalities will they connect with? I strongly encourage you to go out of your way to learn as much as possible about your partners' (and associates') skills and expertise. Otherwise, you will miss opportunities to be genuinely helpful to clients and contacts. I built a fairly good client base as an associate simply by introducing people in my network to skilled lawyers in my firm who could help the clients solve a problem or do a deal.

It also helps you be a resource if you or your firm can produce industry-focused legal or business advisories that are relevant and succinct. Forwarding advisories (or even "articles of interest") can be a simple, but important, way to be a resource (and show you care).

Obstacles to Great Service and Communication

Initially, when I ask lawyers to list what gets in the way of providing extraordinary service to clients, the answers are that they don't have enough time, the compensation system of the firm emphasizes billable time over client satisfaction, and there is a lack of firm or partner support for service initiatives. Inevitably, they put the blame and responsibility on someone or something other than themselves.

After an effective client-service training program, however, those same lawyers admit that it was mostly a lack of understanding or appreciation for the client's point of view, and a failure to understand the importance of client service that got in the way. But even after these apparent and real obstacles have been identified, many attorneys still fall back into old habits. Why?

Awareness of obstacles and a willingness to change are not always enough to help some lawyers alter the way they approach client relationships. Inadequate training and education in communication and service skills for lawyers, and a failure to understand different personality types and communication styles limit the potential for improvement.

And Then There Are the Personalities

The type of person drawn to the legal profession tends to be someone who prefers working alone, using lots of hard, detailed data, and thinking logically about getting to a solution. Once most attorneys have gathered sufficient data and have had enough time to think about it, they want to get to closure.

This is fine when the attorney and the client have the same personality and decision-making type, but that is seldom the case. Most attorneys either do not understand or do not want to bother learning how to accommodate clients' varying communication styles, but top rainmakers do this instinctively. Many lawyers believe deeply that their intellectual and technical skills can and should be sufficient to impress clients. Why, therefore, would they bother learning difficult relationship-building concepts?

Lawyers who learn and apply some relatively simple communication skills involving observation, listening, and communication are often surprised when they see that these skills are practical, manageable, and effective. These skills include well-established practices such as "matching" and "mirroring" a client's body posture, speaking pace, and voice modulation;

and they include "meeting management" (setting an agenda that respects the differences in participant learning behavior and communication preferences), as well as the form of delivery for information (written, graphic, or audio).

It takes a concerted effort to understand and employ these skills. The personal styles and professional expectations that many lawyers bring with them to the practice of law (some would call it "baggage") can only be changed with ongoing individual coaching and support.

Something about going to law school and passing the bar caused many of us to think we are somehow extraordinary. Indeed, we have gained an extraordinary understanding of the law and how to do the technical things that lawyers do—without that you have no clients to serve. But when it comes to being an *extraordinary lawyer*, it is not enough to rely on our great legal educations or how smart we are; it's about the way we treat people and communicate with them.

Conclusion

On the opening page of Wayne Dyer's intriguing book *You'll See It When You Believe It*, I was struck by the following words: "You cannot *drink* the word *water*... The word *rain* cannot get you *wet*... You must experience water or rain to truly know what the words mean." While this may seem obvious, I think we often let ourselves get lulled into the comfort of words. Unfortunately, as Dyer said, "Words themselves keep you several steps removed from the experience."

Let's think about some of the words that have been featured in these pages: communication, responsiveness, accessibility, partnering, value, and service. You might **say** you provide good "value" and "service," or that you are "communicating" well and "partnering" with your clients. But saying these words does not mean that you are actually doing these things, or that your clients are experiencing the hoped-for impact.

How can we say we communicate with our clients when most of us do not even communicate very well with each other? How can we say we deliver "value" or provide excellent "service" when we don't even know how our clients define those terms?

> What a shame it would be to invest time and effort in being a great lawyer, only to miss the point of what matters most to those you are trying to impress. (Essentially, you can end up doing the wrong things for the right reasons.)

How can we claim to be moving toward "partnering" relationships when we have not been to many of our clients' offices in over a year? How can we say we understand our client's business or personal challenges when we have never met their boss or read their strategic plan?

What we think we are doing and achieving and what clients think we are doing and achieving often differ. What we think our role is in the clients' business, and what clients think our role should be, sometimes are not in sync. We must open up the lines of communication to get alignment.

If you are a great lawyer in your clients' eyes, you will have a steady stream of new and repeat business from them, and a regular flow of referral work from the people they refer to you. If you are not getting a flood of repeat, new, and referral work, then you are probably doing something wrong. Great lawyers almost always get the first call whenever someone needs any help with a business or legal challenge.

If you *are* getting a lot of repeat business, new business, and referrals from your clients, you must remain vigilant. Take note of what you are doing for that client, and make sure you continue to do it. Think about the indicia of greatness discussed in this book, and consider whether there is even more you might be able to do to distinguish yourself from other lawyers. Moreover, you should think about how to do for other clients what you are doing for those with whom you work best.

I once saw a poster in a very successful lawyer's office that I found to be rather motivational. It went something like this: "Every morning, a gazelle wakes up knowing that it must outrun the fastest lion or it will be killed. Every morning, a lion wakes up knowing that it must run faster than the slowest gazelle or it will starve. So it doesn't matter whether you are a gazelle or a lion, when the sun comes up, start running!"

Although I started by saying that this book is just a lot of common sense, the behaviors discussed here are not all that common. It takes hard work to be a good lawyer; it takes just a little more work to be a great lawyer. So start running.

It takes time to go to a client's place of business more often and to talk to them about what they need and value. If you are uncomfortable talking to clients, it takes time to get some training or coaching that will help you be more comfortable. You might have to go out of your way to read what your clients read, and to learn what is important to them personally and professionally. If you are unwilling to make the effort to super-satisfy your clients, then you should not be surprised if they become someone else's clients.

A good friend of mine, the president of a Fortune 50 company, was asking me about the types of client-service training programs I do for lawyers. He happens to be one of those no-nonsense, cut-to-the-chase guys. His advice to me was that I should simply tell lawyers to talk to their clients. That sounds like a great idea.

Lawyers who want to succeed should neither accept nor adopt an attitude of "business as usual." Find the will to adopt the broader set of behaviors that are being demanded by the marketplace. Doing so will provide you with a more satisfying and rewarding professional experience.

Find thirty minutes every week to sit quietly and check your performance against the suggestions made in this book. Did you call a client you have not heard from for a while? Did you schedule a client satisfaction discussion with a key client? Did you deliver documents on time this week? (If not, have you apologized?) Did you send a personal note or a gift to any client? Did you thank a referral source?

Challenge yourself to be the best lawyer your clients have ever worked with. Seek out training and coaching if you need it to be extraordinary.

Thank you for letting me share my observations and ideas with you. Together, let's start the process of eliminating lawyer jokes!

About The Author

Jim Durham lives in Dedham, Massachusetts. Jim has been the Chief Marketing Officer of a leading national law firm, coached hundreds of lawyers, and he has consulted with dozens of law firms for over a decade. He is the co-editor and contributing author of *The Lawyer's Guide to Marketing Your Practice, Second Edition*, published by the American Bar Association. He is an engaging, high-energy retreat speaker, who can address all of the topics discussed in this book, as well as Work/Life Balance issues.

Inquires to the author should be sent to jdurham@lfdg.com. Also, this book can be ordered at www.greatlawyeringbook.com.

Jim would like to thank his friend Kevin Armbruster (a truly great lawyer) for giving him the idea for this book.

Notes

<u>Notes</u>

Notes

<u>Notes</u>

Notes

Notes

<u>Notes</u>

Notes

Notes

Notes

<u>Notes</u>